# Preface

IF you are a busy p_____
spare for hobbies, bu_____
to produce your own_____
start you thinking. As you read it, and try out its really
easy recipes, you will begin to wonder why on earth
it has taken you so long to discover this simplest-of-all
method of winemaking, a system which is at once
cheap, easy, and convenient, involving the minimum
of time and labour.

Before writing this book I experimented with one
or two of the more obvious canned fruits—orange, peach,
apricot—and the experiments proved so successful that
I was stimulated to go ahead and try some of the less
likely ingredients to be found on the shelves at the
grocer's or supermarket. A whole new field of all-the-
year-round winemaking opened up, and I was delighted
with the ease and success with which one can use the
various forms of preserved fruit. Consequently I went on
to cover the whole range—it was surprisingly wide—and
this book records the results.

With its aid you will be able to make wine, winter and
summer, from tinned fruit, fruit pulps, pie fillings,
bottled fruit, tinned and bottled juices, syrups and concentrates, jams and jellies, and dried fruit. And you will
be astonished at the ease with which you will turn out
a whole range of attractive wines.

Thinking of having a go? Nip down to that supermarket right away!

C. J. J. BERRY

Published by The Amateur Winemaker
Publications Ltd., Andover, Hants.

SBN 0 900841 00 1

*First impression* 1968
*Twenty-third impression* 1981

Cartoons by Rex Royle
Cover design by George Hodgson

PRINTED IN GREAT BRITAIN BY
STANDARD PRESS (ANDOVER) LTD., ANDOVER, HANTS.

# Winemaking with Canned and Dried Fruit

by

## C. J. J. BERRY

*Editor, The Amateur Winemaker*

A comprehensive guide to the easy production of quality wines from ingredients readily obtainable at supermarket or chemist: tinned fruits, fruit pulps, juices, concentrates, syrups, jams, jellies and dried fruits

AN AMATEUR WINEMAKER PUBLICATION

# CONTENTS

# CONTENTS

# CHAPTER I

# Why Use Preserved Fruit?

WHY make wine from canned fruit? Or from canned or bottled juices? Or from concentrated juices? Or from dried fruit?

If you are a newcomer to winemaking the idea of using anything other than fresh fruit (preferably free!) may at first seem a little bizarre, but as your enthusiasm for winemaking develops—as it will—you will want to make wine the whole year round and not just when a particular fruit is in season. Fresh fruit of good quality is, of course, the ideal winemaking material, but tinned and otherwise preserved fruits also have many advantages, and will certainly make excellent wines. This book sets out to show you how.

Winemaking from preserved fruits and juices opens up a whole range of winemaking activity the whole year round, and the beauty of the system is its convenience, simplicity and cheapness; your ingredients are there ready prepared for you, on the shelves of your supermarket or grocer: they are already cleaned, sliced or chopped, and are invariably of high quality, probably better than you would be able to obtain if growing your own fresh fruit, or buying it from your greengrocer. Quality in tinned fruit, for example, is constant and, better still, there is no waste, no wearisome scrubbing, scraping or peeling; the whole of the fruit you buy can be directly used in your winemaking, and you thus get full value for the small sums of money you expend. Cost is low, rarely more than £1.50 a gallon, or 25p a bottle (for fruit). To this, of course, must be added the cost of the sugar, but that you would usually have to buy whether your ingredients were fresh or canned.

Winemaking from tinned or bottled fruits is certainly convenient; all it usually involves is opening a can of fruit, pulping it, pouring boiling water over it, and over the requisite amount of sugar, adding acid, tannin, yeast and nutrient when it cools, fermenting on the pulp for a short period, and then straining and making the volume up to one gallon. The wine is then fermented out in the usual way, under an air lock. The method is simple, clean and convenient, involving the minimum amount of preparation and "kitchen work", and one can quickly have a whole range of wines, some from the most exotic materials, fermenting.

Some tropical or Far Eastern fruits are unlikely to be available in this country in their fresh form—guavas, lychees and paw paw, for instance—but they can be bought in tins. Often, too, fruits which are obtainable fresh are comparatively expensive—e.g. peaches and pineapples—yet can be purchased quite cheaply tinned.

"That's all very well," I can hear you saying, "but surely I'll have to use a lot of tins to make one gallon of wine? And that'll be expensive." Not at all. Since the whole contents of the can are used and since the average can contains but very little syrup, you will find that, very generally speaking, 1–2 lb. ($\frac{1}{2}$–1 kilo) of fruit will make 1 gallon (4$\frac{1}{2}$ litres) of wine.

Exactly how much fruit has to be used in a particular case, of course, depends upon (a) the strength of flavour of the fruit being used, and (b) the strength of flavour desired in the finished wine. Some fruits, like raspberry, have a very strong flavour, and one can use minimal quantities of them, so that a 15 oz. (500 gms.) tin is adequate for 1 gallon (4$\frac{1}{2}$ litres); other fruits, like pineapple or gooseberry, have a delicate flavour, and two or even three tins of the same size may be necessary.

Happily, however, the modern trend is away from the more strongly flavoured wines and towards the more delicate ones, and this is in our favour, for one can produce light, delicate wines of excellent flavour by using only small quantities of fruit.

The point to remember here is that the use of a reliable wine yeast to protect that delicate flavour becomes all the more important, as does the inclusion of sufficient nutrient, acid and tannin to give a sound fermentation despite the low fruit content. A vigorous but "non-wine" yeast may ferment your must, but may convey off-flavours to your wine in the process, so that its delicate bouquet and flavour will be lost. A "must" with insufficient nutriment for the yeast, or insufficient acid or tannin, may not support a sound fermentation, and all sorts of troubles may arise. So use a reliable *wine* yeast, and sufficient nutrient, acid and tannin.

5

And be careful to give the wine adequate "body" by the inclusion of a little honey, grape concentrate or malt extract, or by the use of glycerine (see page 30) obtainable from any chemist. You will then produce sound light wines of impressive character.

A visit to your grocer's will reveal that there are three main categories of preserved fruit that we can employ for winemaking (we are disregarding deep frozen fruit as too expensive). They are:

1. Tinned and bottled fruit, as whole fruit, purees, or pie fillings.

2. Tinned and bottled juices, concentrates and syrups.

3. Dried fruit.

This book deals with them separately, in that order. The full list of fruits thus available may surprise you. It is:

CANNED: Apples, Apricots, Blackberries, Blackcurrants, Cherries (red and black), Figs, "Fruit Cocktail", "Fruit Salad", Gooseberries, Grapefruit, Greengages, Guavas, Loganberries, Lychees, Melon (cubes), Mango (slices), Oranges (segments), Oranges (Mandarin), Paw Paw (cubes), Peaches (slices, halves or white), Pears, Pineapple (chunks, pieces, rings and pulp), Prunes, Raspberries, Rhubarb and Strawberries. In North America one can also obtain Blueberries, Black Raspberries, Black Bing Cherries, Pitted Red Cherries and Prune Plums.

CANNED PIE FILLINGS: Apple, Bilberry, Blackberry and Apple, Blackcurrant and Apple, Blackcurrant, Cherry, Plum, Gooseberry, Raspberry and Strawberry.

6

CANNED JUICES: Apple, Grapefruit, Orange (natural and sweetened), Pineapple, Tangerine.

CONCENTRATED JUICES: Blackcurrant (Ribena), Cherry, Grape (red and white), Raspberry, Rosehip (frozen), Orange and Rosehip (bottled), Orange (frozen), Grapefruit (frozen).

DRIED FRUIT: Apples, Apricots, Bananas, Bilberries, Cherries, Currants, Dates, Elderberries, Figs, Peaches, Peel, Prunes, Raisins, Rosehips (and shells), Mixed Dried Fruit, Sloes and Sultanas.

# CHAPTER II

# Winemaking Terms

IT has already been necessary to touch briefly upon general winemaking and before going further it would perhaps be as well, for the benefit of the newcomer to this exciting craft, to explain some of the terms which are commonly used.

AEROBIC FERMENTATION: A fermentation conducted in the presence of air, usually the first part of the fermentation process.

ANAEROBIC FERMENTATION: A fermentation from which air is excluded; the second part of the fermentation process.

BALANCE: A wine is said to be "balanced" when flavour, alcohol, sweetness, acidity and astringency are present in the correct proportions, making an harmonious whole.

BLENDING: Mixing finished wines in calculated quantities so that their qualities complement one another to produce a balanced (q.v.) wine. An over-acid wine can be blended with an under-acid one, a harsh wine with an insipid one, a strong wine with a weak one. and so on. One can blend to improve (a) flavour; (b) strength; (c) colour; (d) acidity; (e) degree of dryness or sweetness; (f) degree of acidity; (g) degree of astringency; (h) bouquet—or all eight!

BODY: The fullness of a wine.

CAMPDEN TABLETS: Useful in winemaking for various sterilisation or purification purposes. They supply sulphur dioxide in convenient form.

CARBON DIOXIDE: The odourless, colourless gas given off by a fermenting liquor.

CUP: An American measure, the equivalent of 8 fl. oz or $\frac{1}{2}$ lb. in the case of sugar.

DRY: A wine is said to be dry when all the sugar in it has been used up by the fermentation: it is also said to have "fermented right out."

EQUIPMENT: The joy of winemaking from tinned and dried fruit is that you need the minimum of equipment: a $1\frac{1}{2}$–2 gallon polythene bucket (N.B.polythene and polyethylene are the same), a 1 gallon saucepan or boiler, a nylon flour strainer, a 9 inch polythene funnel, one or two glass 1 gallon jars or jugs (with ear handles), two fermentation locks, and five or six feet of rubber tubing $\frac{3}{8}$ inch diameter. A hydrometer helps, but it not essential. You will also need a supply of wine yeast, yeast nutrient, citric acid and Campden tablets, all of which will make many gallons of wine. Everything else you will already have in your kitchen—including that all-important can-opener!

FERMENTING (or "Working"): The process brought about by yeast acting upon sugar to produce alcohol and carbon dioxide.

FERMENTATION TRAP (or Air Lock): A little gadget used to protect the fermentation from infection.

FINING: Removing suspended solids from a cloudy wine by filtering or adding wine finings.

FLOGGER: A wooden tool for banging corks home.

FORTIFICATION: Increasing the strength of wine beyond that possible by natural fermentation by adding spirit.

GALLON: (*see* page 32).

HYDROMETER: An instrument for measuring the weight (or sugar content) of a liquid.

HYDROMETER JAR: The jar in which a hydrometer is floated for a reading to be taken.

LEES: The deposits of yeast and solids formed during fermentation.

LIQUOR: The unfermented, sugar-containing liquid which will eventually be wine.

MALO-LACTIC FERMENTATION: A tertiary fermentation in the bottle which has the effect of converting malic acid to lactic acid, often rendering the wine less acid.

MUST: The pulp or combination of basic ingredients from which a wine is made.

NUTRIENT: Nitrogenous matter added to the liquor to boost the action of the yeast; yeast food, particularly important when making wines with only small quantities of fruit. It can be bought in tablet form—use 1 tablet per gallon—or you can buy ammonium phosphate from your chemist and use 1 level teaspoon per gallon.

PECTIC ENZYMES: Preparations sold under various trade names (Pectinol, Pektolase, etc.), which break down the pectin content of the fruit and thus improve the extraction of juice and flavour and the making of clear wine. This, it will be noted, is the exact opposite of what is required in jam making, where pectin is added to make the jam "set". Use of a pectin-destroying enzyme is particularly necessary with such fruits as apricot, peach and plum.

PROOF: Proof spirit contains 57.1% alcohol. 70 deg. proof really means 70% of "proof". Thus ordinary proprietary bottles of spirit will contain only 40% alcohol by volume (70% of 57.1%).

RACKING: Siphoning the wine off the lees to clear and stabilise it. An essential part of the winemaking process if "off" flavours are to be avoided. All that is really needed for racking is 4–5 (1½–2m) feet of rubber tubing (⅝ inch diameter). One end is lowered gently into the wine to two or three inches above the yeast deposit. Carry the other end down to a clean jar at a lower level, being careful not to kink the tube. Hold it lightly in place and suck gently at the lower end (very pleasant!) until the wine starts to flow, then direct it into the lower jar. As the level in the upper jar drops push the tube lower but be careful not to suck up any sediment.

STABLE: A wine is said to be stable when there is no danger of further fermentation. If a wine persistently refuses to attain this state, fermentation can usually be terminated by one or more of the following means: Repeated rackings at monthly intervals, the addition of 1 or 2 Campden tablets per gallon, filtering, the addition of spirit (vodka or gin) to raise the alcohol content, or

13

siphoning the wine on to the lees of another wine which has fermented out quickly. One can also buy proprietary wine stabilisers, which should be used in accordance with the suppliers' instructions.

STOPPER: A cork or polythene bottle closure with a projecting cap.

STRAINER: For straining solids from the must. A fine nylon flour sieve or fine mesh nylon net, even a (washed!) nylon stocking will do at a pinch.

SYRUP: Sugar is often added to the must in syrup form, since the addition of solid sugar can sometimes arrest or prevent fermentation. 2 lb. of sugar dissolved in 1 pint of boiling water makes 2 pints of syrup.

TABLESPOON: The British tablespoon equals four British teaspoons and five American teaspoons.

TANNIN: Gives a wine that desirable "bite", zest or astringency. It can be added in the form of proprietary grape tannin—$\frac{1}{4}$–1 teaspoon to a gallon—and can also be obtained by soaking tea leaves, oak leaves, apple or pear peelings, or oak chips in a wine, in which case one can only judge effect by tasting repeatedly.

TEASPOON: An American teaspoon holds four-fifths of the same ingredient as its British equivalent.

VINEGAR: Wine which has "gone wrong" or acetified.

YEAST: The organism which brings about fermentation. It "feeds" on the sugar to obtain the energy for self-reproduction, and by-products of this process are the alcohol we seek and carbon dioxide, the bubbles in your wine or beer.

14

# CHAPTER III

# Theory of Winemaking

FROM reading the foregoing vocabulary you will already have more than a glimmer of an idea what winemaking is all about, and since in this book I am dealing only with one particular kind of winemaking—from tinned and dried fruit, and juices—I do not want to recapitulate a lot of general winemaking theory which you can better read in other books in this series, notably *First Steps in Winemaking* (£1.00) and *Progressive Winemaking* (£1.75).

## YEAST

For our purpose it is sufficient to note that wine, whether "true" wine produced from the juice of grapes, or "wine" produced from the juices of other fruits, is the result of the fermentation of sugar-containing, slightly acidic, liquids by yeast, a minute living organism. It is the yeast which is the true winemaker!

When we extract the flavour from our chosen fruit by pressing, by the use of a juice extractor, or by steeping the fruit in hot or cold water, add sugar and water, and introduce yeast, it "feeds" upon the sugar to obtain the energy for self reproduction, and immediately starts to multiply, its presence making the liquid go "milky". As it uses up the sugar, a gas, carbon dioxide, is produced, together with an equal weight of alcohol, and this process continues until so much alcohol has been produced that the yeast can continue no longer; it stifles in its own by-products, as it were, and this is said to be the limit of its tolerance. Usually this is when about 15 parts in every 100 of the liquid are alcohol, and the wine is thus 15% alcohol by volume.

Often some air is allowed access to the first part of the fermentation, since the oxygen assists the yeast to get going quickly, but after four or five days it is advisable to fit an air lock to the fermentation vessel and cut off the yeast's air supply, for more alcohol is produced by an anaerobic fermentation than an aerobic one.

For the yeast to ferment a liquid well it must have (a) warmth, (b) sugar, (c) acid, (d) nutrient, and (e) oxygen, and all of these we take care to supply. We start our fermentation off in a warm (about 70° F., 21° C.) place for a few days and for the secondary fermentation continue at normal room temperature (60° F., 16° C.).

The sugar we add in the form of household sugar, either beet or cane, made into a syrup.

Nutrient for the yeast—it plays the same role as fertiliser does in your garden, and enables the yeast to work to maximum capacity—is particularly important when using recipes which call for only small quantitites

16

17

of fruit per gallon, for one must ensure that the must contains adequate food for the yeast. Wine yeasts require the same foods as other plants or forms of life: they must have vitamins (of the B complex, aneurine or thiamine) nutrient salts such as ammonium sulphate, ammonium phosphate, potassium phosphate and magnesium phosphate, and certain amino acids. This nutriment is usually most simply provided by employing one of the many excellent proprietary yeast foods obtainable from wine suppliers: they are quite cheap and accompanied by full instructions. Or you can buy ammonium phosphate from your chemist and use 1 teaspoon per gallon, (5 gms to $4\frac{1}{2}$ litres).

Acid is best added in the form of citric acid—a jar can be purchased quite cheaply from your chemist—since this is both more convenient and more easily measured than the old way of using lemons, which is the same chemically. Tannin is best added in the form of one of the excellent proprietary grape tannins which one can now purchase from wine supplies firms.

## FERMENTATION

Having compounded our must (the fruit pulp or juice plus the syrup) we add to it our chosen yeast and nutrient, and in order to extract the full flavour ferment "on the pulp", either in a fermentation jar closed with a cotton wool plug, or in a polythene bucket closely covered with several thicknesses of cloth, to allow some oxygen access whilst at the same time excluding the possibility of airborne infection. The best temperature at this stage is about 70° F. (21° C.).

After this initial aerobic fermentation, which can last anything between four days and three weeks, we strain

18

the liquid into a fermentation jar and make sure that it is full to the bottom of the neck by topping up with cold boiled water. Then a fermentation lock is fitted and the anaerobic, or secondary fermentation is allowed to continue.

The best temperature for this is 60–65° F. (16–18° C.), but this is not critical. Fermentation will proceed steadily if there are no marked drops in temperature and then, gradually, the wine will start to clear, from the top down.

## RACKING

When the top two-thirds are clear, the wine should be racked into a fresh jar, leaving the bulk of the yeast deposit and traces of fruit debris behind, and a fermentation lock fitted again. Racking (*see* "Wine Terms") is most important, both for the preservation of the flavour unspoilt, and for assisting the wine's stabilisation. After racking always "top up" with cold boiled water to fill 1 gallon jar to bottom of neck.

After another two months or so have passed another yeast deposit will have formed and the wine will be completely clear. It should then be racked again and then left to mature for three or four months, preferably in a temperature of 50–55° F., before drinking, but, again, temperature is not critical.

## FINING

Should your wine (after sufficient opportunity) not clear satisfactorily or not have the brilliance you desire, "fine" it by using one of the excellent proprietary finings now on the market. Bentonite is one of the best. For one gallon of wine add ¼ level teaspoon to 1 tablespoon of water, mix thoroughly, and allow to stand for

19

24 to 48 hours. During this time the Bentonite will swell considerably and the mixture become of porridge-like consistency. Stir in a little water (or wine) and add to the main bulk of the wine. Mix thoroughly and put aside to stand for several days. The Bentonite will gradually settle down, leaving the wine clear. It may be then siphoned off and the lees filtered to avoid wastage.

So the general procedure is:

1. Dissolve the sugar you decide to use in half to two-thirds of the water, bringing it briefly to the boil (or use the standard syrup (p. 14) brought to the boil).

2. Strain any syrup from the tin into your fermenting jar.

3. Mash the fruit in the tin and pour it into your polythene bucket. Pour the boiling syrup over it.

4. Allow to cool to 70° F. add acid, tannin, depectinising enzyme, yeast nutrient; stir well.

5. Pour through large funnel into fermenting jar; add yeast. Shake well. Fit air lock.

6. Stand in a warm place (70° F.). Shake well daily; continue for up to 14 days, topping up with remainder of water once the first vigorous fermentation has ceased.

7. Strain into clean fermentation jar, top up with strong syrup to bottom of neck; refit trap; ferment out (65° F.).

8. When wine clears, rack; repeat two months later, this time into clean bottles. Fine if necessary. Store at 50° F.

# CHAPTER IV

# Achieving a Balanced Wine

ALWAYS the aim of the winemaker must be to achieve a well-balanced wine which does not offend our susceptibilities because one aspect of it dominates too much.

In any wine there will be present a basic flavour (of the grape or fruit from which it is made), alcohol, to give it its strength, sweetness, to a greater or lesser degree, acidity and astringency. The wine must also have a vinous quality, of course, a pleasant bouquet and sufficient "body" or substance for its particular purpose. All these characteristics and qualities can vary, and it is this variation which gives both the commercial wine world and the home wine maker such a fascinatingly wide range of wines, from those such as the delicate, slightly flavoured, light Moselles and Hocks, through to the sturdier white wines to the heavier Sauternes and Madeiras. The variation is perhaps even more striking in red wines.

What is not always appreciated is that whatever type of wine is being made, the correct balance should be observed between flavour, strength, sweetness, acidity and astringency, and as a very general rule it can be said that they increase proportionately.

Thus a wine which has but a slight flavour will preferably be not too strong, not too sweet, not too astringent and not too acid, and if any of these *is* too strong, the wine will seem out of balance, but if one is making stronger-flavoured wines—which can be done by using more fruit per gallon—then, generally speaking, one will also need to increase their strength and their sweetness, and perhaps their acidity as well. The attainment of this satisfactory balance is the hall-mark of a good wine.

FLAVOUR, above all, raises important points when one is making wines from tinned fruits or juices. Most of the recipes in this book will produce light wines of the type which are increasingly popular nowadays, and this is an advantage in that they can be made with only very small quantities of fruit. Usually not more than two 15 oz. tins are required to make a gallon of wine, and in the case of strong flavoured fruits only one is often sufficient.

The important thing, when using such small quantities of fruit, however, is to extract the maximum flavour, so when fermenting on the pulp we must do so for as long as is possible without risking off odours. Another way of ensuring maximum extraction is to use Pektolase or some similar pectic enzyme to break down the fruit tissues. It can be added to a cold must at the rate of

1 level tablespoon to the gallon and will ensure a good extraction and a clear wine, but the enzyme must not be used in conjunction with boiling water, which will destroy it. If you have used boiling water or syrup, wait until the must is cold before adding your enzyme, just as you would with your yeast.

When, after a few days, you come to strain the liquid you will find that the pulp residue jellifies, and it will be necessary to roll it to and fro on some nylon mesh, or rotate it in a nylon sieve.

Another critical factor in obtaining a good flavour is your yeast. Always use a reliable, true wine yeast. Baker's yeast or wild yeasts will, of course, give a fermentation, but when we are making delicate-flavoured wines it is important that a true wine yeast should be used, so as to preserve the nuances of flavour undamaged by the "off" tastes and odours which are often introduced by baker's yeasts or wild yeasts. Wild yeasts are everywhere about us, in the air, on plants, in our mouths, and can invade and spoil our wines unless they are protected, and that is why our musts should be sterilised by boiling or with boiling water, and why, after our chosen yeast has been introduced, ferments should be protected by means of an air lock.

A wine yeast has three main advantages; it will preserve a delicate flavour unspoilt, it will give just that little extra alcohol, and it will usually give a firm sediment which makes racking easier and less wasteful.

"Your bottle of Gin made an excellent fortifier"

Many types of pure wine yeast, cultured under laboratory conditions, are now available—Port, Sherry, Madeira, Tokay, Burgundy, Bordeaux, Bernkasteler, Graves, Hock, etc.—but all the names mean is that they have been cultured from the bloom of the grapes in that particular region, and are therefore suitable for making wines of the type for which that region is noted. Obviously, it is best to employ a yeast in a must which will be "sympathetic" to it, red wine yeast in a red wine, white wine yeast in a white, a champagne yeast in a sparkling wine, and so on, but if you are using wine yeasts for the first time, and have no strong preferences, your best bet is to ask your winemaking supplier for a "General purpose wine yeast."

If wine yeast is unobtainable, 1 level teaspoon per gallon of granulated yeast may be used, but in this case be particularly careful to rack as soon as a thick deposit has formed.

And since the fruit content of your wines is likely to be low, always remember to include a good proprietary nutrient for the yeast.

STRENGTH: A rough rule of thumb is that 1 lb. of sugar *in* the gallon will give you 5% of alcohol. Most wines are between 10% and 15% alcohol, and if the yeast were always to use up all the sugar one could thus hope to make with 3 lb. sugar wines of 15% alcohol by volume which were dry, with no residual sugar. Sugar over and above that level merely remains in the wine as a sweetener, since the yeast cannot use it up.

In practice, however, things do not always work out this way, and if one wishes to be certain of having a dry wine one usually requires not more than 2¼ lb. of sugar *in* the gallon. Note the difference between *in* the gallon and *to* the gallon; if you are adding sugar *to* a gallon of water you will require 2 lb. 9 oz. to achieve the same result, and will finish up with 1 gallon 25 fl. oz. of must because of the added bulk of the sugar.

In other words, if you put 2¼ lb. of sugar in a gallon jar, and fill up with liquid, you have 2¼ lb. *in* the gallon, not added *to* a gallon, a distinction that is often overlooked.

For dry wines, then, 2¼ lb. of sugar *in* the gallon, for medium wines 2 lb. 10 oz. in the gallon, and for really sweet wines 3 lb. 4 oz. in the gallon.

For those who wish to use a hydrometer (see *First Steps in Winemaking*), the respective specific gravities are 1085, 1100 and 1125, as will be seen from the table on the next page. For the convenience of N. American readers the Brix or Balling Scale is given as well as the S.G. one. The gallons mentioned in the last three columns are Imperial or British gallons.

The sugar is best used in the form of syrup which can be heated and poured over the mashed fruit to extract the flavour. It is convenient if only a portion of the gallon of water—say half a gallon—is used to dissolve the sugar, because the fruit will also occupy a little bulk, and the jar should always later be topped up with more water to give an exact gallon of fermenting must.

| S.G. | Degrees Brix or Balling | Potential % alcohol by volume | Amount of sugar in the gallon lb. oz. | | Amount of sugar added *to* the gallon lb. oz. | | Vol. of one gallon with sugar added gal. fl. oz. | |
|------|------|------|------|------|------|------|------|------|
| 1010 | 3.0  | 0.9  |   | 2  |   | 2½ | 1 | 1  |
| 1015 | 4.3  | 1.6  |   | 4  |   | 5  | 1 | 3  |
| 1020 | 5.5  | 2.3  |   | 5  |   | 8  | 1 | 5  |
| 1025 | 6.8  | 3.0  |   | 7  |   | 10 | 1 | 7  |
| 1030 | 8.0  | 3.7  |   | 12 |   | 13 | 1 | 8  |
| 1035 | 9.2  | 4.4  |   | 15 | 1 | 0  | 1 | 10 |
| 1040 | 10.4 | 5.1  | 1 | 1  | 1 | 2  | 1 | 11 |
| 1045 | 11.6 | 5.8  | 1 | 3  | 1 | 4  | 1 | 13 |
| 1050 | 12.8 | 6.5  | 1 | 5  | 1 | 7  | 1 | 14 |
| 1055 | 14.0 | 7.2  | 1 | 7  | 1 | 9  | 1 | 16 |
| 1060 | 15.2 | 7.8  | 1 | 9  | 1 | 11 | 1 | 17 |
| 1065 | 16.4 | 8.6  | 1 | 11 | 1 | 14 | 1 | 19 |
| 1070 | 17.6 | 9.2  | 1 | 13 | 2 | 1  | 1 | 20 |
| 1075 | 18.7 | 9.9  | 1 | 15 | 2 | 4  | 1 | 22 |
| 1080 | 19.8 | 10.6 | 2 | 1  | 2 | 6  | 1 | 23 |
| 1085 | 20.9 | 11.3 | 2 | 4  | 2 | 9  | 1 | 25 |
| 1090 | 22.0 | 12.0 | 2 | 6  | 2 | 12 | 1 | 27 |
| 1095 | 23.1 | 12.7 | 2 | 8  | 2 | 15 | 1 | 28 |
| 1100 | 24.2 | 13.4 | 2 | 10 | 3 | 2  | 1 | 30 |
| 1105 | 25.3 | 14.1 | 2 | 12 | 3 | 5  | 1 | 32 |
| 1110 | 26.4 | 14.9 | 2 | 14 | 3 | 8  | 1 | 33 |
| 1115 | 27.5 | 15.6 | 3 | 0  | 3 | 11 | 1 | 35 |
| 1120 | 28.5 | 16.3 | 3 | 2  | 3 | 14 | 1 | 37 |
| 1125 | 29.6 | 17.0 | 3 | 4  | 4 | 1  | 1 | 38 |
| 1130 | 30.6 | 17.7 | 3 | 6  | 4 | 4  | 1 | 40 |
| 1135 | 31.6 | 18.4 | 3 | 8  | 4 | 7  | 1 | 42 |

To calculate how much space will be occupied by any given quantity of sugar plus water remember that any number of pounds of sugar, dissolved in half that number of pints of water, will produce the same number of pints of syrup as they were pounds of sugar, and each pint will naturally contain 1 lb. of sugar.

Thus:

| Sugar (lbs.) | | Water (pints) | | Syrup (pints) |
|---|---|---|---|---|
| 8 | + | 4 | = | 8 (1 gallon) |
| 4 | + | 2 | = | 4 (½ gallon) |
| 2 | + | 1 | = | 2 (¼ gallon) |

SWEETNESS: This, too, is naturally determined by the amount of sugar which one adds and there is consequently always liable to be confusion over the correct amount to use. It is easy enough to make a dry wine, in which all the sugar will be used up during fermentation, and it is all too easy to produce a strong, oversweet wine which has far too much residual sugar after fermentation has finished. What is difficult to produce is a medium wine of the correct degree of sweetness. The practical solution is to ignore sugar for sweetening purposes, and use it solely for the purpose of producing alcohol. Use only sufficient sugar (2½ lb. in the gallon at most) to produce a dry wine, and then sweeten the finished wine to taste, at the same time stabilising it by adequate racking and maturation, and possibly by the addition of 1 Campden tablet per gallon or a proprietary stabilising agent. Some wine-makers like to use Lactose (milk sugar) for this final sweetening, since it is not fermentable by the yeasts we use and therefore will not cause further fermentation in the bottle, but this is unnecessary if one takes the suggested precautions.

ACIDITY: Dry wines should have about 5 parts per thousand acid and sweet wines 7 parts per thousand, and in most of the recipes in this book this will be best obtained by the addition of $\frac{1}{4}$–$\frac{1}{2}$ oz. of citric acid. The amount required will vary according to the acidity of of the fruit being used, naturally. For instance rhubarb, Morello cherries, gooseberries, raspberries, are high in acidity; grapes, apples and plums are "normal", and figs and dates are low.

TANNIN: Some of the ingredients recommended, —notably the red fruits, pears, and apples—have sufficient tannin, but in most of the recipes in this book the wine will be found to be better for the addition of a little grape tannin, as recommended, since only small quantities of fruit are employed.

BODY: For the same reason—that we are using only minimal quantities of fruit—our wines will tend to be thin, or lacking in "body". If you have two liquids, one thin like water and one thick like glycerine, and both have neither taste nor smell but contain the same quantity of acid, the "thin" liquid will tend to seem more acid than the "thick". This is because, like sugar, the thickness of the liquid acts as a buffer between the acid and one's tastebuds. Wines made with "normal" quantities of fruit and sugar will probably contain enough buffering agents to make the acid level required for good fermentation tolerable, but wines made with minimal quantities of fruit or juice and sugar may taste both over-acid and over-dry, or harsh. The remedy for this is to add more body by substituting for $\frac{1}{2}$ lb. of the total sugar recommended in any recipe $\frac{1}{2}$ lb. of honey, $\frac{1}{2}$ lb. of malt extract, or 1 pint of grape concentrate,

according to taste. From the flavour point of view honey and grape concentrate are generally preferable, but malt extract has the advantage that it will usually ensure a rapid fermentation. This substitution, of course, is done when the wine is being made. If a *finished* wine is slightly over-acid or harsh, this can be remedied by the cautious addition of small quantities of glycerine (do not overdo it—one teaspoon at a time per bottle) stirred well in. If the wine is very acid, of course, remedial treatment with acid-reducing solution may be necessary.

American readers should note that they can use the recipes in this book with ease to produce in each case 1 gallon (U.S.). Since the pound measure of weight is the same in both countries, and since the quantities of fruit advocated are small, it is quite practical, where can sizes differ, to use the nearest size if the exact British size quoted is unobtainable.

The only alteration to make is in the quantity of sugar. Since the American gallon is one-sixth smaller (128 liquid ozs., or 231 cubic inches, compared with the Imperial gallon's 160 liquid ozs., or $277\frac{1}{4}$ cubic inches) it is necessary to use only five-sixths the amount of sugar used in the British gallon, working to the nearest quarter pound, and then to make one (U.S.) gallon. Quantities of principal ingredients can be left unchanged.

Measurements are given in *level* British teaspoons and tablespoons, and four teaspoons equal one tablespoon. The American "tablespoon" is only half the size of the British, and the American teaspoon is smaller than the British one and holds only four-fifths of the same ingredient, so for "1 tablespoon" American readers should substitute five teaspoons.

## CHAPTER V

# Tinned and Bottled Fruit

MOST of the tinned fruits with which we deal in the following recipes are obtainable in at least seven sizes of can, but there are many variations between makes.

The usual sizes are:—

> 5 oz.
> 8 oz.
> 10 oz.
> 15½ oz.   (AIT)
> 1 lb. 3 oz.   (A2)
> 1 lb. 12 oz.   (A2½)
> 6 lb.   (A10)

and the sizes which will best suit our purpose are generally the 15½ oz., for making one gallon of dry wine, and the 1 lb. 12 oz. can when making sweet wines which require a stronger flavour.

American sizes were being changed as this book was being written, and new sizes are given in parentheses;

common sizes available (all in fluid ounces) are: 10, 15 (14), 20 (19) and 28 fl. oz. The most convenient size to substitute for the British 15½ oz., it will be found, is the 19 fl. oz.

The dry wines are generally made with 2¼ lb. of sugar in the gallon and the sweet with 3¼ lb. in the gallon.

In making some wines, notably those from stone fruit, the use of a pectin-destroying enzyme such as Pektolase is desirable to assist flavour extraction and prevent pectin hazes. The pectin enzyme is added when the must has cooled, and is then given 24 hours to do its work before the yeast is added. This we call in the recipes Method "A", as used for Apricot wine.

Where no pectic enzyme is necessary, the yeast and nutrient are added as soon as the must is cool, and this we call Method "B", as used for Blackberry.

Smooth the wines finally by the careful addition of glycerine, if necessary.

## APPLE WINE (Dry)

| | Metric |
|---|---|
| 1 lb. 12 oz. tin of apple pulp (U.S. 28 fl. oz.) | 1 kilo |
| 2¼ lb. sugar (U.S. 1 lb. 14 oz. | 1 kilo |
| 1 tablespoon depectiniser (U.S. 2 tablespoons) | 15 mls |
| 1 Campden tablet | |
| 2 level teaspoons citric acid | 10 mls |
| 1 yeast nutrient tablet | |
| Sherry yeast | |
| Water to 1 gallon | 4½ litres |

This wine is best made by the cold water method, to avoid the "cooked" flavour which appears when boiling water is used. Crush the Campden tablet and then pour all the ingredients except the yeast through a funnel into your fermenting jar and pour in two quarts of cold water. Stir vigorously with an oaken rod for several minutes to dissolve the sugar. Fit air lock. Next day add your yeast, shake jar vigorously, and refit lock. Leave for ten days in a warm place, shaking jar vigorously each day. Then strain into fresh jar, top up to bottom of neck with water and refit trap. Leave to ferment out, racking and bottling as usual. For a sweet wine increase sugar content to 3¼ lb. or top up with standard syrup instead of water.

## APRICOT WINE

|  | *Metric* |
|---|---|
| 15 oz. tin apricot pulp or halves or slices (U.S. 19 oz.) | 500 gms |
| 2¼ lb. sugar (U.S. 1¾ lb.) | 1 kilo |
| 1 teaspoon citric acid | 5 ml |
| 1 tablespoon depectiniser (U.S. 2 tablespoons) | 15 ml |
| 1 teaspoon tannin | 5 ml |
| 1 yeast nutrient tablet | |
| Sauternes yeast | |
| Water to 1 gallon | 4½ litres |

If using halves, mash the fruit with a stainless steel spoon, having poured any syrup into your fermenting jar. Then use Method "A":

Boil two quarts of water and dissolve the sugar in it, then put pulp into polythene bucket and pour the boiling syrup over it. Allow to cool to tepid (70° F.) before adding acid, tannin, and depectiniser. Stir well, cover closely, and leave in a warm place. Next day stir, pour the whole into the fermenting jar with the syrup from the can, and add yeast, nutrient, and enough cold water to bring level of must to just below the shoulder of the jar, leaving room for a "head". Fit air lock and leave in a warm place for ten days, shaking jar daily to disperse pulp through liquid. Then strain into a fresh jar, and top up to bottom of neck with water. Ferment out, racking and bottling as usual. For a sweet wine use a 1 lb. 12 oz. tin of pulp and 3¼ lb. (U.S. 2¾ lb.) of sugar.

## BILBERRY WINE

|  | Metric |
|---|---|
| 1 lb. bottle or 15 oz. tin bilberries (or whortleberries) | 500 gm |
| 2¼ lb. sugar (U.S. 1¾ lb.) | 1 kilo |
| ½ teaspoon tannin | 2.5 ml |
| 2 teaspoons citric acid | 10 ml |
| 1 tablespoon depectiniser | 15 ml |
| (U.S. 4 teaspoons) | |
| 1 nutrient tablet | |
| Bordeaux yeast | |
| Water to 1 gallon | 4½ litres |

Bilberries (or whortle berries, from *Vaccinium Myrtillus*, a small shrub about 18 inches high) are obtainable in 1 lb. bottles or 15 oz. tins (sold as pie fillings) and they make a superb red wine. Strain off any syrup into your fermenting jar, and crush the fruit in a basin with a stainless steel spoon. Bring five pints of water to the boil, and then add the sugar. Stir well. Add the bilberries and simmer for not more than six minutes, then allow to cool. Pour into fermenting jar through a funnel, and add the crushed nutrient tablet, the citric acid, the tannin, depectiniser and yeast. Shake well, and fit air lock. Keep in a warm place, and shake the jar daily for ten days. Strain the liquor off through a nylon sieve or net, rolling from side to side to make the pulp jellify, and return to cleaned fermenting jar, which should be topped up

**"HAROLD!"**

with water to bottom of neck and have the trap refitted. Ferment out, rack, and bottle in the usual way.


## BING CHERRY (see CHERRY)


## BLACKBERRY WINE

|                                   | Metric    |
| --------------------------------- | --------- |
| 15 oz. tin blackberries           | 500 gms   |
| 2¼ lb. sugar (U.S. 1¾ lb.)        | 1 kilo    |
| ¼ teaspoon tannin                 | 1 ml      |
| 1 nutrient tablet                 |           |
| Bordeaux yeast                    |           |
| Water to 1 gallon                 | 4½ litres |

This is Method "B": Pulp the blackberries and pour over them the syrup made by dissolving the sugar in two quarts of boiling water. Allow to cool, then pour the whole into a fermenting jar, and add the syrup from the tin, the crushed nutrient tablet, the citric acid, tannin, and yeast. Add a little cold water to bring level to shoulder, shake vigorously, and then fit air lock. Ferment on the pulp in a warm place for ten days or so, shaking the jar each day, then strain into fresh jar, top up to the bottom of neck with syrup, fit air lock, and ferment out. Rack when wine clears, and again two months later. Keep fermenting jar away from the light or the wine may lose its glorious colour. For a sweet wine use two 15 oz. tins and 3¼ lb. sugar (U.S. 2¾ lb.).

# BLACKBERRY AND APPLE

|                                         | *Metric*     |
|-----------------------------------------|--------------|
| 15 oz. tin blackberry and apple puree   | 500 gms      |
| 2¼ lb, sygar (U,S, 1¾ lb,)              | 1 kilo       |
| 1 teaspoon citric acid                  | 5 ml         |
| ¼ teaspoon tannin                       | 1 ml         |
| 1 tablespoon depectiniser               |              |
|     (U.S. 2 tablespoons) | 15 ml   |
| Bordeaux yeast                          |              |
| 1 nutrient tablet                       |              |
| Water to 1 gallon                       | 4½ litres    |

Not all pie fillings on the market are suitable for winemaking, for some of them contain only a tiny portion of actual fruit and a large amount of other ingredients to give both bulk and setting qualities. We found this to be the case with two leading brands. Others are reasonably satisfactory; it all depends on the actual fruit content. Unfortunately, one cannot tell which type one has until the tin is opened, so the only solution is to leave until then the decision as to whether one makes wine—or a pie!

If the fruit content is adequate, at least 60% of the bulk, stick to the above recipe, but if it is very low, use two cans instead of one. A handful of fresh elderberries or other red fruit will improve the colour of red wines, which is apt to be bluish and poor, and the use of Pectozyme is absolutely essential.

Empty the can into a basin and pour over the fruit two kettles (two quarts) of boiling water. Stir well. Funnel the sugar into your fermenting jar and when the pulp has cooled to about 70° F. pour it all in on top of the sugar, add the depectiniser, acid and tannin, and stir vigorously with an oaken rod to dissolve sugar. Stopper lightly with cotton wool. Leave for 24 hours in a warm place, then add crushed nutrient tablet and wine yeast.

Fit air lock, ferment for 10 days, then strain into clean fermenting jar and top up with syrup to bottom of neck. Refit air lock, ferment out, and rack and bottle as usual.

## BLACKCURRANT AND APPLE

Another pie filling sold in 15 oz. tins. Method as for Blackberry and Apple.

## BLACKCURRANT WINE

|  | *Metric* |
|---|---|
| 15 oz. tin blackcurrants | 500 gms |
| 3¼ lb. sugar (U.S. 2¾ lb.) | 1.5 kilo |
| ½ teaspoon citric acid | 2.5 ml |
| ½ teaspoon tannin | 2.5 ml |
| 1 tablespoon depectiniser (U.S. 2 tablespoons) | 15 ml |
| 1 yeast nutrient tablet | |
| Bordeaux yeast | |
| Water to 1 gallon | 4½ litres |

Blackcurrants are a highly acid fruit, but since we are using only a small quantity we still need to add a little citric acid to obtain a balanced must. The flavour is also strong, so this is best made as a sweet wine. Dissolve the sugar in five pints of boiling water, and simmer the crushed fruit for about ten minutes. Cool, add the acid, tannin and depectiniser, and pour all into the fermenting jar, and fit air lock. Twenty-four hours later introduce the yeast and nutrient, refit lock and ferment on the pulp for 10 days away from the light to preserve colour. Strain into clean fermenting jar, filling to bottom of neck with water, and refit air lock. Ferment out, rack and bottle as usual.

## BLUEBERRY

Blueberry (or Blaeberry: the American *Vaccinium Corymbosum*, a shrub which grows to 8 ft. high). As for Bilberry. 19 fl. oz. size tin per gallon.

**"It's Blackberry and Apple Liqueur"**

# CHERRY WINE

|                                  | Metric        |
|----------------------------------|---------------|
|                                  | *Metric*      |
| Two 14 oz. tins black cherries   | 1 kilo        |
| 2¾ lb. sugar                     |               |
|    (U.S. 2¼ lb.)  | 1¼ kilo       |
| 1 teaspoon citric acid           | 5 ml          |
| 1 yeast nutrient tablet          |               |
| Wine yeast                       |               |
| Water to 1 gallon                | 4½ litres     |

Both black and red cherries, which are sold in 14 oz. tins, are best used for making medium wine (2¾ lb. sugar) or sweet wine (3¼ lb. sugar) and to get a really satisfactory flavour one needs two tins. One can also buy 15 oz. tins of cherry pie filling.

They contain quite a lot of pectin (like most stone fruit) so it is important to use depectiniser, and they are also a little low in acid.

Method: As for bilberries.

# CHERRIES (Morello, Choke or Montmorency)

|                                  | Metric        |
|----------------------------------|---------------|
|                                  | *Metric*      |
| 2 lb. jar Morello cherries       | 1 kilo        |
| 2½ lb. sugar                     |               |
|    (U.S. 2 lb.)   | 1¼ kilo       |
| 1 tablespoon depectiniser        |               |
|    (U.S. 2 tablespoons) | 15 ml   |
| ½ teaspoon tannin                | 2.5 gm        |
| 1 nutrient tablet                |               |
| Yeast                            |               |
| Water to 1 gallon                | 4½ litres     |

Bring five pints of water to the boil and simmer the cherries in it for five minutes. Turn them into a poly-thene bucket, allow them to cool, and then mash well by hand to release the stones. Add the depectiniser, cover, and leave for 24 hours. Then strain into fermenting jar, stir in the sugar, tannin, nutrient and yeast, and top up with water to just below neck. Fit trap and ferment out, rack and bottle as usual.

## FRUIT COCKTAIL

|  | *Metric* |
|---|---|
| 15 oz. tin fruit cocktail | ½ kilo |
| 2¼ lb. sugar (U.S. 1¾ lb.) | 1 kilo |
| 1 teaspoon citric acid | 5 ml |
| 1 teaspoon tannin | 5 ml |
| 1 tablespoon depectiniser (U.S. 2 tablespoons) | 15 ml |
| 1 yeast nutrient tablet |  |
| General purpose wine yeast |  |
| Water to 1 gallon | 4½ litres |

These tins of mixed fruit are sold as "fruit salad" or as "fruit cocktail". Basically they are the same, containing peaches, pears, pineapple and (the occasional!) cherry. The "cocktail" tin also includes grapes. The fruit salad consists of fruit whole or in chunks; the fruit cocktail is usually diced. Both can be used to make a pleasant white wine.

The method is the same for both. The syrup is strained out of the can into a fermenting jar and the fruit is put through a liquidiser (remove cherry stone first) or mashed with a stainless steel spoon in a basin. Thereafter use Method "A". For a sweet wine use two tins of fruit and 3¼ lb. of sugar (2¾ lb. U.S.).

## GOOSEBERRY WINE

|  | Metric |
|---|---|
| 1 lb. 4 oz. tin gooseberries<br>(or 15½ oz. tin of gooseberry pie filling) | ½ kilo |
| 2½ lb. sugar<br>(U.S. 2 lb.) | 1¼ kilo |
| 1 tablespoon depectiniser<br>(U.S. 2 tablespoons) | 15 ml |
| 1 nutrient tablet |  |
| Wine yeast |  |
| Water to 1 gallon | 4½ litres |

Crush the gooseberries by hand in a polythene bucket, and pour over them the boiling syrup made by dissolving the sugar in two quarts of water. Thereafter continue with method "A", as for Apricot.

## GRAPEFRUIT WINE

|  | Metric |
|---|---|
| 1 lb. 3 oz. tin of grapefruit segments | ½ kilo |
| 2½ lb. sugar<br>(U.S. 2 lb.) | 1¼ kilo |
| 1 teaspoon tannin | 5 ml |
| 1 yeast nutrient tablet |  |
| Wine yeast |  |
| Water to 1 gallon | 4 litres |

This fruit is sufficiently acid to enable one to omit any citric acid from the recipe. Method "B", as for Blackberry.

44

"Gooseberry, Elderberry, or Tea?"

# GRAPEFRUIT AND MAYFLOWER

(An "every day" wine for making in quantity).
To make five gallons:

| | Metric |
|---|---|
| 5 tins grapefruit (family size) | 5 kilos |
| ½ gallon mayflowers | 2 litres |
| 3 lb. raisins | 1½ kilos |
| 9 lb. sugar (U.S. 7½ lb.) | 4 kilos |
| 1 tablespoon tannin | |
| (U.S. 2 tablespoons) | 15 ml |
| ½ oz. tartaric acid | 15 gm |
| 4 nutrient tablets | |
| Sauternes yeast | |
| 5 gallons boiled water | 23 litres |

Boil up the sugar in the water and pour on to the crushed fruit. Allow to cool, add all the other ingredients, and ferment on the pulp, closely covered for 14 days, stirring daily, then strain off into air locked fermentation vessel or vessels.

# GREENGAGE WINE

| | Metric |
|---|---|
| 2¼ lb. tin greengages (2¼ lb.) | 1 kilo |
| 2½ lb. sugar | |
| (U.S. 2 lb.) | 1¼ kilo |
| 1 teaspoon tannin | 5 ml |
| 1 tablespoon depectiniser | |
| (U.S. 2 tablespoons) | 15 ml |
| 1 nutrient tablet | |
| Wine yeast | |
| Water to 1 gallon | 4½ litres |

Greengages make an excellent wine and the one produced by the above recipe will be dry. For a sweet wine use two 1 kilo tins—for some reason or other the only tins I have been able to find have been 1 kilo— and 3¼ lb. of sugar (U.S. 2¾ lb.). Greengages have sufficient acid, but, like most stone fruit, may be difficult to clear unless depectiniser is used. Method "A", as for Apricot.

# GUAVA WINE

|  | Metric |
|---|---|
| Three 14 oz. tins of guavas | 1½ kilos |
| 2¼ lb. sugar | |
| (U.S. 1¾ lb.) | 1 kilo |
| 2 teaspoons citric acid | 10 ml |
| 1 teaspoon tannin | 5 ml |
| 1 nutrient tablet | |
| 1 tablespoon depectiniser | |
| (U.S. 2 tablespoons) | 15 ml |
| Wine yeast | |
| Water to 1 gallon | 4½ litres |

This fruit makes an agreeable table wine with a pleasant but not overpowering bouquet. Method "A", as for Apricot.

# JAM or JELLY WINE

|  | Metric |
|---|---|
| 4 lb. jelly or jam, any flavour or combination (U.S. approximately 36 fl. oz.) | 2 kilos |
| 1¼ lb. sugar | |
| (U.S. 1 lb.) | ½ kilo |
| 1 tablespoon depectiniser | 15 ml |
| (U.S. 2 tablespoons) | |
| (or 1/10th oz. 10 x strength pectic enzyme) | |
| 2 teaspoons citric acid | |
| (3 if using fruit low in acid) | 10 ml |
| 1 teaspoon tannin | 5 ml |
| Yeast and nutrient | |
| Water to 1 gallon | 4½ litres |

First day: Pour five pints boiling water over the jelly or jam and allow to cool overnight.

Second day: Add the depectiniser, cover, and allow to stand for three days. Prepare yeast starter.

Fifth day: Strain the must back into a saucepan and boil for five minutes. Pour boiling liquor on to the sugar and allow to cool. Adjust gravity if necessary to

47

about 90. Add citric acid, tannin, nutrient, and yeast. Pour into fermenting jar, top up with water to bottom of neck, and place in warm place. After third day fit air lock and continue as usual.

## FIG WINE

| | Metric |
|---|---|
| Two 1 lb. 3 oz. tins of figs | |
| (U.S. two 16 fl. oz.) | 1 kilo |
| 2¼ lb. sugar | |
| (U.S. 1¾ lb.) | 1 kilo |
| 1 tablespoon citric acid | |
| (U.S. 2 tablespoons) | 15 ml |
| ½ teaspoon tannin | 2.5 ml |
| 1 tablespoon depectiniser | |
| (U.S. 2 tablespoons) | 15 ml |
| 1 yeast nutrient tablet | |
| General purpose wine yeast | |
| Water to 1 gallon | 4½ litres |

Method "A", as for Apricot.

## LOGANBERRY WINE

| | Metric |
|---|---|
| 15 oz. tin loganberries | ½ kilo |
| 2¾ lb. sugar | 1¼ kilo |
| (U.S. 2¼ lb.) | |
| ½ teaspoon citric acid | 2.5 ml |
| 1 tablespoon depectiniser | 15 ml |
| 1 nutrient tablet | |
| Wine yeast | |
| Water to 1 gallon | 4½ litres |

One tin and the above sugar will suffice for a light dry wine, but to my mind this is a more satisfactory wine made as a sweet one with two tins of fruit and 3¼ lb. sugar (U.S. 2¾ lb.). There is no need to increase the acid, since loganberries have plenty of it. Method "A", as for Apricot.

# LYCHEE WINE

|  | Metric |
|---|---|
| 1 lb. 4 oz. tin of Lychees | ½ kilo |
| 2¾ lb. sugar | |
| (U.S. 2¼ lb.) | 1¼ kilo |
| 1 tablespoon depectiniser | |
| (U.S. 2 tablespoons) | 15 ml |
| 2 teaspoons citric acid | 10 ml |
| ½ teaspoon tannin | 2.5 ml |
| 1 nutrient tablet | |
| Wine yeast | |
| Water to 1 gallon | 4½ litres |

Method "A", as for Apricot. A pleasant, medium wine of delicate flavour, clean to the taste.

# MANDARIN ORANGES

|  | Metric |
|---|---|
| 15 oz. tin of mandarin oranges | |
| (U.S. two fl. oz. tins | ½ kilo |
| 2½ lb. sugar | |
| (U.S. 2 lbs.) | 1¼ kilo |
| ½ teaspoon citric acid | 2.5 ml |
| 1 teaspoon tannin | 5 ml |
| 1 nutrient tablet | |
| Sauternes yeast | |
| Water to 1 gallon | 4½ litres |

This can be made as either a dry or a sweet wine; for a sweet wine increase the sugar to 3¼ lb. (U.S. 2¾ lb.). Method "B", as for Blackberry.

## MELON CUBES

|  | Metric |
|---|---|
| Two 1 lb. 3 oz. tins of melon cubes | 1 kilo |
| 2½ lb. sugar | 1¼ kilo |
| 2 teaspoons citric acid | |
| (U.S. 1 tablespoon) | 10 ml |
| 1 teaspoon tannin | 5 ml |
| 1 nutrient tablet | |
| Chablis yeast | |
| Water to 1 gallon | 4½ litres |

Because of the delicate flavour of the cubes at least two tins are necessary and with the above ingredients produce a light dry table wine of the hock type. Method "B", as for Blackberry.

## MANGO WINE

|  | Metric |
|---|---|
| 16 oz. tin mango slices | ½ kilo |
| 2½ lb. sugar | |
| (U.S. 2 lb.) | 1¼ kilo |
| 2 teaspoons citric acid | 10 ml |
| 1 teaspoon tannin | 5 ml |
| 1 tablespoon depectiniser | |
| (U.S. 2 tab espoons) | 15 ml |
| 1 nutrient tablet | |
| Sauternes yeast | |
| Water to 1 gallon | 4½ litres |

This is another attractive light golden table wine, best made as a dry wine. Method "A", as for Apricot.

## ORANGE WINE

|  | Metric |
|---|---|
| 15 oz. tin orange segments | ½ kilo |
| 2½ lb. sugar | |
| (U.S. 2 lb.) | 1¼ kilo |
| ½ teaspoon citric acid | 2.5 ml |
| 1 teaspoon tannin | 5 ml |
| 1 nutrient tablet | |
| Sauternes yeast | |
| Water to 1 gallon | 4½ litres |

**ORANGE, Mandarin** (*see* pages 49–50)

## PAW PAW WINE

|  | Metric |
|---|---|
| 15½ oz. tin paw paw cubes | ½ kilo |
| 2¼ lb. sugar | |
| (U.S. 2 lb.) | 1¼ kilo |
| 2 teaspoons citric acid | 10 ml |
| 1 teaspoon tannin | 5 ml |
| 1 nutrient tablet | |
| General purpose wine yeast | |
| Water to 1 gallon | 4½ litres |

This is a fruit low in acid and astringency, but which in a balanced must produces an excellent dry white wine. It will also make a pleasant dessert wine if two tins are used instead of one, and the sugar is increased to 3¼ lb. (U.S. 2¾ lb.). Use Method "A", as for Apricot.

## PEACH WINE

|  | Metric |
|---|---|
| 15½ oz. or 16 oz. tin peach slices | |
| (U.S. 19 fl. oz.) | ½ kilo |
| 2¼ lb. sugar | |
| (U.S. 2 lb.) | 1¼ kilo |
| 1 teaspoon citric acid | 5 ml |
| 1 tablespoon pectic enzyme | |
| (U.S. 2 tablespoons) | 15 ml |
| ½ teaspoon tannin | 2.5 ml |
| 1 nutrient tablet | |
| Sauternes wine yeast | |
| Water to 1 gallon | 4½ litres |

The peaches can be bought in slices in either 15½ oz. or 16 oz. tins, as halves in 16 oz. tins, or labelled "white peaches" in 16 oz. tins. Wine firms also sell peach pulp. One 15½ oz. or 16 oz. tin of either will make, using the quantities in the recipe, a light dry table wine, but if a fuller-bodied wine is required use two tins of peaches (roughly 2 lb.)—they are quite cheap—and increase the sugar to 2¾ lb. (U.S. 2¼ lb.), the citric acid to 2 teaspoons, and the tannin to 1 teaspoon. Use Method "A", as for Apricot.

## PEAR WINE

|  | Metric |
|---|---|
| Two 15½ oz. tins pears | |
| (U.S. 28 fl. oz.) | 1 kilo |
| 2¼ lb. sugar | |
| (U.S. 1¾ lb.) | 1 kilo |
| 2 teaspoons citric acid | 10 ml |
| ½ teaspoon tannin | 2.5 ml |
| 1 nutrient tablet and wine yeast | |
| Water to 1 gallon | 4½ litres |

Crush the fruit or put it in a liquidiser to make it into a purée before putting it into your polythene bucket and pouring the hot syrup over it. Continue with Method "B", as for Blackberry.

## PINEAPPLE WINE

|  | Metric |
|---|---|
| 15 oz. tin pineapple chunks or rings | |
| (U.S. 19 fl. oz.) | ½ kilo |
| 2¼ lb. sugar | |
| (U.S. 1¾ lb.) | 1 kilo |
| 2 teaspoons citric acid | 10 ml |
| ½ teaspoon tannin | 2.5 ml |
| 1 nutrient tablet | |
| Wine yeast | |
| Water to 1 gallon | 4½ litres |

It is immaterial what form of tinned pineapple is used, but the absolute minimum is a 15 oz. tin, and one can if desired use two since the flavour is delicate. Both pineapple chunks and pineapple rings can be purchased in 8½ oz., 12 oz. and 15 oz. tins, and crushed pineapple

"But it distinctly says DRIED Pineapple Rings . . ."

or pineapple pulp can be bought in 15½ oz. or 1 lb. 12 oz. tins, respectively. (The large tin will make two gallons of very light wine or one of medium body; the latter is preferable.)

For a dessert wine use two 15 oz. tins and 1 lb. more sugar.

If using pineapple chunks or rings they should be finely chopped or put through a liquidiser to reduce the particle size and assist extraction. Thereafter use Method "B", as for Blackberry.

## PLUM WINE

|  | *Metric* |
|---|---|
| 1 lb. 3 oz. tin of plums | ½ kilo |
| 2¼ lb. sugar<br>    (U.S. 1¾ lb.) | 1 kilo |
| 2 teaspoons citric acid | 10 ml |
| 1 tablespoon depectiniser<br>    (U.S. 2 tablespoons) | 15 ml |
| 1 nutrient tablet | |
| Bordeaux yeast | |
| Water to 1 gallon | 4½ litres |

Either golden or red plums are suitable and can be bought in 1 lb. 3 oz. or 6 lb. tins. One can also buy plum pulp in 1 lb. 12 oz. tins and canned plum pie fillings, both of which are also suitable for winemaking, so this is a good cheap wine to make in quantity at any time of the year.

Plum wine is notoriously difficult to clear unless a pectin destroying enzyme is used, so follow method "A" as for Apricot.

# PRUNE WINE

|  | Metric |
|---|---|
| 15½ oz. tin prunes | ½ kilo |
| 2½ lb. sugar | |
| (U.S. 2 lb.) | 1¼ kilo |
| 2 teaspoons citric acid | 10 ml |
| 1 tablespoon depectiniser | |
| (U.S. 2 tablespoons) | 15 ml |
| ½ teaspoon tannin | 2.5 ml |
| 1 nutrient tablet | |
| Wine yeast | |
| Water to 1 gallon | 4½ litres |

Follow Method "A". This makes a good general-purpose wine, particularly useful for blending purposes.

# PRUNE PLUMS

As plum: use two 14 fl. oz. tins per gallon.     1 kilo

# RASPBERRY WINE

|  | Metric |
|---|---|
| 15½ oz. in raspberries | ½ kilo |
| 2½ lb. sugar | |
| (U.S. 2 lb.) | 1¼ kilo |
| 1 nutrient tablet | |
| Bordeaux yeast | |
| Water to 1 gallon | 4½ litres |

Raspberries are available in a range of tin sizes—8 oz., 10 oz., 13½ oz., 15½ oz., and 1 lb. 3 oz., but the 15½ oz. is the minimum for 1 gallon of medium wine, using the quantities above. One can also buy tins of raspberry pie fillings which are eminently suitable for winemaking. Raspberries are among the most acid of fruits, and both citric acid and tannin can be omitted. To our mind an even more attractive wine results by doubling the quantity of fruit and increasing the sugar to 3¼ lb. (U.S. 2¾ lb.) to make a sweet wine. Use Method "B", as for Blackberry.

# RHUBARB WINE

| | Metric |
|---|---|
| Two 1 lb. 3 oz. tins of rhubarb | 1 kilo |
| 3 lb. sugar | |
| (U.S. 2½ b.) | 1½ kilo |
| 1 tablespoon depectiniser | |
| (U.S. 2 tablespoons) | 15 ml |
| 1 nutrient tablet | |
| White wine yeast | |
| Water to 1 gallon | 4½ litres |

Here a cold water method must be used or you are likely to run into jellification troubles. Chop, crush or mince the rhubarb, conserving the juice, or put it through a liquidiser, and then pour the cold water on to it and add the pectozyme, and 1 Campden tablet. Stand in a warm place closely covered for 24 hours. Then stir in the sugar and add your yeast and nutrient. Cover closely again and leave for four days, stirring daily. Then strain into fermentation jar, top up with water to bottom of neck, and fit air lock. Ferment out rack and bottle as usual.


# ROSEHIP PUREE

| | Metric |
|---|---|
| 15 oz. can puree of Irish rosehips | ½ kilo |
| 5½ lb. sugar | |
| (U.S. 4¾ lb.) | 2½ kilos |
| 2 nutrient tablets | |
| Montrachet wine yeast (or Vierka Tokay) | |
| Water to 2 gallons | 9 litres |

Citric acid is included in the can's contents. Mix all the ingredients together and add enough water to bring the volume to two gallons. Ferment on the pulp for 14 days, then strain into fermenting vessel and fit air lock. A delicious sweet wine: if a dry wine is desired reduce sugar to 4½ lb. (U.S. 4 lb.).

# STRAWBERRY WINE

|  | Metric |
|---|---|
| 15½ oz. tin strawberries | ½ kilo |
| (U.S. two 14 fl. oz.) | |
| 2¼ lb. sugar | |
| (U.S. 1¾ lb.) | 1 kilo |
| 1 tablespoon citric acid | |
| (U.S. 2 tablespoons) | 15 mls |
| ½ teaspoon tannin | 2.5 ml |
| 1 nutrient tablet | |
| Wine yeast | |
| Water to 1 gallon | 4½ litres |

Strawberries can be bought in 7¾ oz., 10 oz., or 15½ oz. tins or as tinned pie fillings, but a 15½ oz. tin is the minimum for making 1 gallon.

Use Method "A".

# CHAPTER VI

# Canned and Bottled Juices and Concentrates

JUICES, like fruits, can be bought in an almost bewildering assortment of sizes in both tins and bottles. As a general rule the most convenient size for our purpose is the 19 oz. one which will in most instances make one gallon of wine, though two tins will be necessary if a strong flavour is desired.

Grapefruit, orange, and pineapple juices can all be bought either sweetened or unsweetened in 19 oz. tins, and apple juice can be purchased in 1 qt. 6 oz. tins which, again, will make a gallon of excellent wine. The only canned juice that I have avoided for winemaking purposes is tomato!

Apple, orange, pineapple and raspberry juices can also be obtained in 3 pint tins costing about 20p, and these will conveniently make two gallons of wine. Even "Welfare" orange juice has been known to be turned unscrupulously into wine!

The natural, unsweetened juices are the best for our purpose and we shall need to use sugar at the rate of 2¼ lb. in the gallon for a dry wine, 2 lb. 10 oz. for a medium wine and 3¼ lb. in the gallon for a really sweet wine which will give us gravities (depending on the fruit) of about 1090, 1105, and 1130 respectively.

When using the sweetened juices we shall need to add less sugar, of course; gravities vary from fruit to fruit, but it is easy to check by means of the hydrometer that one has achieved the correct gravity.

Our recipes are for the use of the natural (unsweetened) juice the use of which is that much less complicated.

Wine can also be made with the greatest ease from the bottled concentrated fruit syrups such as raspberry (17½ fl. oz.), Morello Cherry (17½ fl. oz.)—both of which will make two gallons — and rosehip and blackcurrant (Ribena) can be bought from chemists in 8 oz. and 12 oz. bottles. Robinson's also do a range of really strong syrups in 6 oz. bottles: orange, strawberry, raspberry, and rosehip, any one of which will make a gallon.

And finally, of course, one has the range of grape juice concentrates available from wine firms, which can be used to produce a range of red and white wines of all types.

Nothing could be simpler than using all these juices and concentrates and this method can be employed for all the following recipes except where otherwise stated:

Put all the ingredients, including the activated yeast, into your fermenting jar and run in enough cold water to reach to the shoulder of the jar; leave plenty of space for the first vigorous and usually frothy ferment and stand the jar on a tray just in case! Stir vigorously with an oaken rod to dissolve the sugar. Plug the neck of the jar with cotton wool until the ferment quietens and stand the jar in a warm (70° F.) place for about a week. Give it a vigorous shake each day. At the end of that time the ferment will be a little quieter, so top up to the bottom of the neck with cold water and fit a fermentation trap. Ferment the wine out (about 65° F.), rack when it clears, and repeat the process two months later when a second yeast deposit has been thrown.

## APPLE

|  | Metric |
|---|---|
| 1 Qt. 6 oz. tin apple juice | |
| (U.S. 48 fl. oz.) | 1¼ litres |
| 2½ lb. sugar | |
| (U.S. 2 lb.) | 1¼ kilos |
| 1 nutrient tablet | |
| Yeast | |
| Water to 1 gallon | 4½ litres |

A lighter wine can be produced by making two gallons instead of one from a 3 pint tin, doubling up the quantities of the other ingredients.

## APRICOT

The following recipe (for 10 gallons of wine) uses a £3 tin of concentrate (7 lb. 6 oz.) and makes a superb dessert wine.

Empty pulp into a container (or containers) and add 20 lb. sugar. Boil seven gallons of water and pour this over the pulp and sugar. Stir well until the sugar dissolves.

"I'll take this one."

When lukewarm add yeast, nutrient and 2 oz. citric acid. Ferment for two weeks, then add another 10 lb. sugar which has been dissolved previously in a gallon of boiling water and allowed to cool.

Make up to 10 gallons with cool water (which has been boiled). Leave to ferment. The liquid may be siphoned occasionally to remove the sediment.


## BLACKCURRANT (*see* "Ribena")


## GRAPE CONCENTRATE

The degree of dilution to be employed when using the concentrated grape juices which are now available depends upon (*a*) the type of wine one wishes to make, and (*b*) the gravity or density of the particular concentrate.

With most of those on the market one can add one, two, two and a half, or even three parts of water to one part of grape juice, and to each gallon add 2 level teaspoons of citric acid. Then the yeast is added and the must fermented in the usual way, whether red or white.

The greater the dilution, of course, the less body the wine will have, and the less strength. It is not really wise to use more than $2\frac{1}{2}$ parts of water to one of grape juice if one is using no added sugar; above this dilution you will certainly need to add sugar if a wine of reasonable strength is to be produced.

For instance, to one gallon of grape juice add 2 gallons of water. To another gallon of water add 4 lb. sugar and $\frac{1}{2}$ oz. tartaric acid. Boil this second lot until all the sugar has dissolved, then add to the grape mixture.

Your hydrometer is the only reliable guide; dilute your concentrate to obtain gravities of 1090 (dry), 1100 (medium) and 1120 (sweet). Most suppliers include full instructions and recipes.

## GRAPEFRUIT

|                              | Metric      |
|------------------------------|-------------|
| 19 oz. tin grapefruit juice  | ½ litre     |
| 2½ lb. sugar                 |             |
| (U.S. 2 lb.)                 | 1¼ kilos    |
| ½ teaspoon tannin            | 2.5 ml      |
| 1 nutrient tablet            |             |
| Yeast                        |             |
| Water to 1 gallon            | 4½ litres   |

If canned juice contains added sugar, use ¼ lb. less sugar. Smooth finished wine with glycerine.

## ORANGE

|                                              | Metric      |
|----------------------------------------------|-------------|
| 19 oz. tin of natural orange juice           | ½ litre     |
| or two 6 oz. Robinson's orange syrup         |             |
| or two 6 oz. bottles "Welfare" orange juice  |             |
| 2½ lb. sugar                                 |             |
| (U.S. 2 lb.)                                 | 1¼ kilo     |
| ½ teaspoon tannin                            | 2.5 ml      |
| 1 nutrient tablet                            |             |
| Yeast                                        |             |
| Water to 1 gallon                            | 4½ litres   |

A 3 pint tin of orange juice will make two gallons of wine, used with double the quantities of the other ingredients in the above recipes.

# ISRAELI ORANGE

|  |  | Metric |
|---|---|---|
| 2 cans Israeli unsweetened orange juice (brands such as Assis) | | 1 litre |
| 1¾ lb. sugar (U.S. 1½ lb.) | | ½ kilo |
| 3 teaspoon depectiniser (U.S. 4 teaspoons) | | 10 ml |
| Grey Owl Tokay yeast | | |
| Nutrient—1 tablet or ½ teaspoon ammonium phosphate | | |
| A Campden tablet or sulphite for 50 ppm. | | |
| Water to 1 gallon | | 4½ litres |

First prepare the yeast starter by taking a sterile wine bottle and pouring into it one of the pint cans of orange juice, topping the bottle up to the shoulder with water and adding the yeast culture and half a teaspoonful of depectiniser. Plug with cotton wool and place in a warm place (around 75° F., 24° C.).

When, on shaking the bottle slightly and holding aslant, a stream of bubbles is apparent, prepare the remainder of the brew as follows. Into a clean gallon jar pour the sugar, yeast nutrient, the other two teaspoonsful of depectiniser and the other can of orange juice. Add half a gallon of water and stir or swirl thoroughly to dissolve the sugar. Do not use hot water or the depectiniser will become denatured. Stand in a warm place for an hour so that the must is the same temperature as the yeast starter. Add the bottle of yeast starter to the main must having first given it a thorough shake, and top up the jar to the shoulder with water (preferably also at 75° F., 24° C.). Fit an air lock or a bored cork plugged with cotton wool.

"Hic! tha's some smashin' Grapefruit Juice Dad's got down there, Mum!"

As soon as fermentation commences increase the temperature gradually up to 85° F., 30° C. Fermentation at this temperature should be complete in 7–10 days. Then add a ground-up Campden tablet or sulphite to 50 ppm. and four days later rack into a clean jar, topping up with water. It is important not to be miserly in racking as any attempt to get the last drop of wine will result in yeast being sucked over. It is better to make the wine in five or ten gallon lots and to rack by gradually lowering the siphon tube down the carboy so that only the final gallon has any sizeable yeast deposit sucked over.

The wine should now be stored in as cool a place as possible until Drinking-day. On D-day the wine has to be racked once more and sweetened following which it is immediately drunk.


## ORANGE SPARKLEY

|  | Metric |
|---|---|
| Two 19 oz. tins commercial orange juice | |
| zest and juice of 2 fresh oranges | 1 litre |
| 1 teaspoon citric acid | 5 ml |
| 50 saccharin tablets | |
| 10 oz. syrup or sugar | 250 ml |
| Wine yeast | |
| Water to 1 gallon | 4½ litres |

Ferment the sugar and orange must to absolute dryness, and then sweeten to taste with saccharin. Prime the brew with about two ounces of concentrated orange squash, and bottle in screw top or crown cork bottles. The solid parts of orange will settle with the yeast and can be re-suspended by gently turning the bottle over before opening. This drink is popular, cheap, harmless, and easy to make.

# MORELLO CHERRY

|  | Metric |
|---|---|
| 17½ fl. oz. tin Morello cherry concentrate | 500 ml |
| 3 lb. sugar | |
| (U.S. 2½ lb.) | 1½ kilo |
| ½ teaspoon tannin | 2.5 ml |
| 1 tablespoon depectiniser | |
| (U.S. 2 tablespoons) | 15 ml |
| 1 nutrient tablet | |
| Yeast | |
| Water to 1 gallon | 4½ litres |

# PINEAPPLE

|  | Metric |
|---|---|
| Two 19 oz. tins pineapple juice | 1 litre |
| 2½ lb. sugar | |
| (U.S. 2 lb.) | 1¼ kilo |
| 1 teaspoon citric acid | 5 ml |
| ½ teaspoon tannin | 2.5 ml |
| 1 nutrient tablet | |
| Yeast | |
| Water to 1 gallon | 4½ litres |

A three pint tin of pineapple juice will make two gallons but the quantities of the other ingredients must be doubled.

# RASPBERRY

|  | Metric |
|---|---|
| (1) 6 oz. bottle Robinson's raspberry con- | |
| centrated syrup | 200 mls |
| 2½ lb. sugar | |
| (U.S. 2 lb.) | 1¼ kilo |
| 1 nutrient tablet | |
| Yeast | |
| Water to 1 gallon | 4½ litres |
| (2) 17½ fl. oz. bottle raspberry syrup or 3 pint tin | |
| raspberry juice | 500 mls |
| 5 lb. sugar | 2¼ kilos |
| 2 nutrient tablets | |
| Yeast | |
| Water to 2 gallons | 9 litres |

# RIBENA (Blackcurrant)

|  | Metric |
|---|---|
| 12 oz. bottle Ribena syrup | 350 mls |
| 3 lb. sugar (U.S. 2½ lb.) | 1½ kilos |
| ½ teaspoon citric acid | 2.5 mls |
| 1 nutrient tablet | |
| Yeast | |
| Water to 1 gallon | 4½ litres |

Before using them stand the bottles of fruit (opened) in a saucepan of water and gradually raise the temperature to 80° C. Hold it there for 10 minutes to drive off any sulphite in the solution.

# ROSEHIP

|  | Metric |
|---|---|
| 12 oz. bottle rosehip syrup | 350 mls |
| 2¼ lb. sugar (U.S. 1¾ lb.) | 1 kilo |
| 1 teaspoon citric acid | 5 mls |
| 1 nutrient tablet | |
| Yeast | |
| Water to 1 gallon | 4½ litres |

# STRAWBERRY

|  | Metric |
|---|---|
| Two 6 oz. bottles Robinson's syrup | 350 mls |
| 2½ lb. sugar (U.S. 2 lb.) | 1¼ kilo |
| ½ teaspoon citric acid | 2.5 mls |
| ⅛ teaspoon tannin | 2.5 mls |
| 1 nutrient tablet | |
| Yeast | |
| Water to 1 gallon | 4½ litres |

"For heaven's sake—how could I get you drunk on
Pineapple Juice?"

**CHAPTER VII**

# Dried Fruit

THERE is a far greater range of dried fruit available for winemaking than most people realise, and much of it is really excellent material. Not only is it cheap, but it is readily available all the year round, and can thus help to spread your winemaking activity evenly through the year. By using dried fruits you can turn out large quantities of wine during the winter months with the greatest of ease.

Look at the impressive list of fruits available in dried form: apples, apricots, bananas, bilberries, cherries, currants, dates, elderberries, figs, grapes (raisins and sultanas), mixed fruit, peaches, prunes, raisins, sloes and sultanas—all of these can be used.

The only general principle that one needs to bear in mind is that generally when using dried fruit the weight required will be only a quarter of that when using fresh fruit, owing to the missing water content.

There are really only two basic ways of using dried fruit:

JUICE METHOD: Here we soak the fruit in about five pints of water for, say, 12 hours, and then bring the whole to the boil and simmer for five to six minutes, thus extracting the flavour. The liquid is then strained off and the sugar stirred into it. Then, when it is cool, it is poured into the fermentation jar and the acid, tannin, nutrient, and yeast added. Usually a little head-space is left at this stage until the fermentation quietens. A week or so later the jar is topped up with cold water and the air lock fitted. Thereafter fermentation and racking, etc., proceed as usual.

PULP METHOD: Is to put the dried fruit, sugar, acid and tannin—but not the yeast and nutrient—into a polythene bucket (or dustbin, for larger quantities) and pour five pints or so of boiling water over them. We use only five pints because the added sugar will fill the remaining portion of our 1 gallon jar later on. The must is stirred well to dissolve the sugar. The yeast and nutrient are added when it has cooled to 70° F. and then one ferments on the pulp for a week in the closely covered bucket, stirring daily. Then the liquor is strained into a glass fermentation jar, which is topped up to the bottom of the neck in cold water, and a fermentation lock fitted. Thereafter proceed as usual.

The only complication is that in some cases depectiniser needs to be employed; this must not be added until the must is cool, and preferably 24 hours before the yeast, so one prepares the must, cools it, adds depectiniser, waits 24 hours, adds yeast and nutrient and then continues as usual.

## APPLE WINE

|  | Metric |
|---|---|
| 2 lb. dried apples | 1 kilo |
| 2¼ lb. sugar | |
| (U.S. 1¾ lb.) | 1 kilo |
| 2 teaspoons citric acid | 10 mls |
| Sauternes or sherry yeast | |
| 1 Campden tablet | |
| 1 tablespoon depectiniser | |
| (U.S. 2 tablespoons) | 15 mls |
| 1 nutrient tablet | |
| Water to 1 gallon | 4½ litres |

Use pulp method, but use cold water instead of boiling and add 1 Campden tablet at the same time as the depectiniser.

## APRICOT

|  | Metric |
|---|---|
| 1 lb. dried apricots | ½ kilo |
| 2½ lb. sugar | |
| (U.S. 1¾ lb.) | 1 kilo |
| 2 teaspoons citric acid | 10 mls |
| 1 tablespoon depectiniser | |
| (U.S. 2 tablespoons) | 15 mls |
| 1 nutrient tablet and yeast | |
| Water to 1 gallon | 4½ litres |

Juice method with depectiniser.

## APRICOT and FIG WINE

|  | Metric |
|---|---|
| 1 lb. dried apricots | ½ kilo |
| 1 lb. dried figs | ½ kilo |
| 1 lb. sultanas or raisins | ½ kilo |
| 2 oz. dried bananas | 60 gms |
| 2¼ lb. sugar | |
| (U.S. 2 lbs.) | 1¼ kilos |
| 2 teaspoons citric acid | |
| (U.S. 1 tablespoon) | 10 mls |
| 1 tablespoon depectiniser | |
| (U.S. 2 tablespoons) | 15 mls |
| 1 nutrient tablet | |
| Sauterns yeast | |
| Water to 1 gallon | 4½ litres |

Chop the dried fruits: thereafter pulp method with pectic enzyme.

## BANANA WINE

|  | Metric |
|---|---|
| 12 oz. packet dried bananas | 350 gms |
| 8 oz. raisins | 225 gms |
| 2¼ lb. sugar | |
| (U.S. 1¾ lb.) | 1 kilo |
| 2 teaspoons citric acid | 10 mls |
| ½ teaspoon tannin | 2.5 mls |
| 1 nutrient tablet | |
| Sherry yeast | |
| Water to 1 gallon | 4½ litres |

Juice method.

## BANANA and ROSEHIP

|  | Metric |
|---|---|
| 4 oz. dried rosehip shells | 125 gms |
| 12 oz. dried bananas | 350 gms |
| 2 teaspoons citric acid | 10 mls |
| 2½ lb. sugar | |
| (U.S. 2 lb.) | 1¼ kilos |
| 1 nutrient tablet | |
| Yeast | |
| Water to 1 gallon | 4½ litres |

Bring three pints of water to boil and pour over the rosehip shells. Simmer the dried bananas in water in a pressure cooker for 10 minutes. Mix the two lots, add half a pint of cold water, and add citric acid and sugar. Stir well. When cool (70° F.) add the yeast starter. Ferment on the pulp for seven days, stirring every day. Strain off into a gallon jar, topping up if necessary with syrup, fit air lock, and continue as usual.

## BILBERRY (or Blueberry) WINE

|  | Metric |
|---|---|
| ½ lb. dried bilberries | 250 gms |
| 2¼ lb. sugar | |
| (U.S. 1¾ lb.) | 1 kilo |
| ½ lb. raisins | 250 gms |
| 1 teaspoon citric acid | 5 mls |
| 1 nutrient tablet | |
| Bordeaux yeast | |
| Water to 1 gallon | 4½ litres |

Pulp method.

## CHERRIES

|  | Metric |
|---|---|
| 1 lb. dried cherries | ½ kilo |
| ½ lb. sultanas | 250 gms |
| (U.S. white raisins) | |
| ½ teaspoon citric acid | 2.5 mls |
| 2¼ lb. sugar | |
| (U.S. 1¾ lb.) | 1 kilo |
| ½ teaspoon tannin | 2.5 mls |
| 1 nutrient tablet | |
| G.P. wine yeast | |
| Water to 1 gallon | 4½ litres |

Juice method. (Soak both cherries *and* sultanas overnight.)

## CURRANT WINE

|                                  | Metric       |
|----------------------------------|--------------|
| 3 lb. currants                   | 1½ kilo      |
| ⅓ lb. mixed minced peel          | 250 gms      |
| ½ lb. barley                     | 250 gms      |
| 3 lb. sugar                      |              |
| (U.S. 2½ lb.)                    | 1½ kilo      |
| 1 teaspoon citric acid           | 5 mls        |
| 1 nutrient tablet                |              |
| Yeast                            |              |
| Water to 1 gallon                | 4½ litres    |

Juice method.


## DATE WINE

|                                  | Metric       |
|----------------------------------|--------------|
| 4 lb. dates                      | 1¾ kilos     |
| 3 lb. sugar                      |              |
| (U.S. 2½ lb.)                    | 1½ kilos     |
| 2 teaspoons citric acid          | 10 mls       |
| ½ teaspoon tannin                | 2.5 mls      |
| 1 tablespoon depectiniser        |              |
| (U.S. 2 tablespoons)             | 15 mls       |
| 1 nutrient tablet                |              |
| Yeast                            |              |
| Water to 1 gallon                | 4½ litres    |

Pulp method with depectiniser.


## DATE and APRICOT

|                                  | Metric       |
|----------------------------------|--------------|
| 2 lb. dates                      | 1 kilo       |
| 1 lb. dried apricots             | ½ kilo       |
| 2½ lb. sugar                     |              |
| (U.S. 2 lb.)                     | 1¼ kilo      |
| 2 teaspoons citric acid          | 10 mls       |
| 1 teaspoon tannin                | 5 mls        |
| 1 nutrient tablet                |              |
| Yeast                            |              |
| Water to 1 gallon                | 4½ litres    |

Juice method with depectiniser.

## ELDERBERRY (as Bilberry)

## FIG WINE

|  | Metric |
| --- | --- |
| 2 lb. dried figs | 1 kilo |
| 2½ lb. sugar | |
| (U.S. 2 lb.) | 1¼ kilo |
| 1 teaspoon tannin | 5 mls |
| 1 nutrient tablet | |
| Wine yeast | |
| Water to 1 gallon | 4½ litres |

Juice method.

## MIXED DRIED FRUIT

|  | Metric |
| --- | --- |
| Three 12 oz. cartons of mixed dried fruit from chain store | 1 kilo |
| 1 lb. wheat | ½ kilo |
| 2¾ lb. sugar | |
| (U.S. 2¼ lb.) | 1¼ kilo |
| G.P. wine yeast | |
| Yeast nutrient | |
| 1 teaspoon citric acid | 5 mls |
| Water to 1 gallon | 4½ litres |

Pulp method.

## MOSS BERRIES (Canadian)

As bilberries or elderberries.

## ORANGE PEEL

|  | Metric |
| --- | --- |
| 1 pint of pieces of dried orange peel | 500 mls |
| ½ teaspoon citric acid | 2.5 mls |
| ½ oz. root ginger | 15 gms |
| ½ lb. raisins | 250 gms |
| 2½ lb. sugar | |
| (U.S. 2 lb.) | 1¼ kilo |
| 1 nutrient tablet | |
| Yeast | |
| Water to 1 gallon | 4½ litres |

Pulp method. Pour the boiling water over the peel and leave for three days. Remove peel and add ginger, raisins, sugar, acid, nutrient and yeast, stir thoroughly and ferment, closely covered for about a week in a warm place. Then strain into fermenting jar, fit air lock, and ferment out as usual. An excellent dry wine with a bite!

## PEACH

|  | Metric |
|---|---|
|  | *Metric* |
| 1 lb. dried peaches | ½ kilo |
| 1 lb. fresh bananas (no skins) | ½ kilo |
| 1 heaped tablespoon dried rose petals | 30 mls |
| 2 lb. white sugar | |
| (U.S. 1¾ lb.) | 1 kilo |
| 1 tablespoon depectiniser | |
| (U.S. 2 tablespoons) | 15 mls |
| 1 teaspoon citric acid | 5 mls |
| 1 teaspoon ammonium phosphate | 5 mls |
| Water to 1 gallon | 4½ litres |

Pulp method: Wash and cut up the peaches and drop them into a clean polythene bucket with the sugar. Pour in 6 pints boiling water and stir till the sugar is thoroughly dissolved, cover and leave to cool then add the depectiniser. Cut the bananas into small portions. Boil these in a pint of water gently for 30 minutes, let it stand to cool, then strain the banana juice into the main juice (don't squeeze the pulp). Cover, leave till next day. Then add the ammonium phosphate, citric acid and wine yeast, previously activated. Stir well and ferment on the pulp for five to seven days, stirring daily. Strain into fermentation jar (don't squeeze the pulp) and make up to just over 7 pints with cold tap water, fit air lock and let fermentation continue until gravity drops to 5 or a little less; then add the rose petals. Refit lock and ferment for a further 7 days. Taste the wine, which will probably be too dry, so add 4 fl. oz. strong sugar syrup every fifth day until you reach the sweetness that suits

you;   then leave the wine a full month undisturbed.
Thereafter rack every two months, until the wine no
longer throws a deposit.

This is an unusually attractive wine well worth making.


# PRUNE WINE

| | Metric |
|---|---|
| 4 lb. prunes | 1¾ kilo |
| 2 teaspoons citric acid | 10 mls |
| 3 lb. sugar<br>(U.S. 2½ lb.) | 1½ kilo |
| ½ teaspoon tannin | 2.5 mls |
| 1 tablespoon depectiniser<br>(U.S. 2 tablespoons) | 15 mls |
| 1 nutrient tablet | |
| Yeast | |
| Water to 1 gallon | 4½ litres |

Pulp method with depectiniser.


# RAISIN WINES
## (Some American recipes)
### Table Wine

| | Metric |
|---|---|
| 3 lb. raisins | 1½ kilo |
| 1¼ gallons water | 5½ litres |
| ¼ oz. tartaric or citric acid | 10 mls |
| 2 Campden tablets | |
| 1 Active Champagne yeast starter | |
| 4 lb. raisins | 1¾ kilo |

Coarsely grind or chop raisins, place in freshly
cleaned crock or cask with head out. For every 3 lb.
raisins pour 1 gallon of water over coarsely ground

raisins, boiling hot; mix gently and let set to cool overnight.

Press lightly through a clean sieve or muslin. Collect juice in clean container.

To lightly pressed raisins add $\frac{1}{4}$ gallon boiling hot water for each 3 lb. raisins used. Mix thoroughly and press once more through muslin, etc. Discard pressed raisins. Combine the pressed juice. 3 lb. raisins should yield about 1 gallon juice.

Now measure or weigh out the tartaric or citric acid and the crushed Campden tablet into about 1 cup or more of water. Stir to dissolve, then add to the prepared juice, mix, leave 4–6 hours or overnight, then introduce yeast and nutrient. When fermented dry, let wine settle for 1–2 weeks then rack and clarify into a freshly cleaned container store at cool temperature (under 60° F.) for 1–2 weeks under fermentation lock. After settling clear, rack off wine into clean bottles and add at this point 1 Campden tablet.

If mellow or slightly sweet taste is desired, add at time of last racking enough sugar to taste then heat sweetened wine to 140° F., bottle, hot cap or cork tightly, keep in cool place for ageing or until consumed.

### Dessert Wine, Sweet

To above recipe add 1 lb. ($\frac{1}{2}$ kilo) sugar to each gallon of prepared juice. Then follow directions for fermenting, settling, clarifying as for table wines. This type of wine can stand again in a clean oak cask after first clarifying and settling as for table wine above.

### California Type Sherry

Use the recipe above for table wines, but increase raisins from 3–4 lb. for every gallon of juice to be

81

prepared. Then follow the directions for fermenting outlined for table wines.


## Spanish Type Flor Sherry

For each gallon of juice use:

|  | Metric |
|---|---|
| ½ oz. pure grade gypsum anhydrous | 15 gms |
| 1 Campden tablet | |
| 1 Active Sherry yeast starter | |
| 3–4 oz. sugar per gallon of juice | 100–120 gms |

Prepare raisin juice as suggested for table wines. Use gypsum in place of tartaric or citric acids and Sherry Yeast Culture in place of Champagne yeast.

When fermentation has been completed, let settle for 1–2 weeks then rack clear wine into glass container or oak barrel, to only three-quarters full. Cover opening of glass container or barrel bunghole with cheese cloth or cotton plug. Store wine at 60°–65° F., not higher, for 3–6 months, during which time a film or flor may develop on the surface of the wine which in turn produces the Sherry character. Do not disturb this film during this period.

When film has grown for 3–6 months or flor character has sufficiently developed the wine may be racked into fresh clean containers, glass or oak barrel to full for further ageing, if desired. At the time of this racking add 1 Campden tablet for each gallon of wine.

## ROSEHIP WINE

|  | *Metric* |
|---|---|
| ½ lb. dried rosehips or 6 oz. rosehip shells | 250 or 180 gms |
| 2½ lb. sugar | |
| (U.S. 2 lb.) | 1¼ kilo |
| 1 teaspoon citric acid | 5 mls |
| ½ teaspoon tannin | 2.5 mls |
| 1 nutrient tablet | |
| Yeast | |
| Water to 1 gallon | 4½ litres |

Pulp method.


## SLOE WINE

(As Bilberry).


## SULTANA SHERRY (White Raisins)

|  | *Metric* |
|---|---|
| 1 lb. sultanas or "white raisins" | ½ kilo |
| 1 lb. grapes | ½ kilo |
| 2½ lb. sugar | |
| (U.S. 2 lb.) | 1¼ kilo |
| 8 oz. barley | 225 gms |
| ½ teaspoon citric acid | 2.5 mls |
| 1 nutrient tablet | |
| Sherry yeast | |
| Water to 1 gallon | 4½ litres |

Soak the barley overnight in half a pint of (extra) water and the next day mince both grain and sultanas. Bring water to the boil and pour it over grain and fruit, then crush the grapes manually and add. Stir in the sugar and make sure it is all dissolved. Allow to cool to just tepid, then introduce the nutrient, acid, and yeast. Ferment closely covered for 10 days, stirring vigorously daily, then strain into fermenting jar and fit trap.

# INDEX

# INDEX

# INDEX

# Other "AW" Books

## SEND FOR OUR CURRENT PRICE LIST

**FIRST STEPS IN WINEMAKING**

The acknowledged introduction to the subject. Unbeatable at the price.

C. J. J. Berry

**SCIENTIFIC WINEMAKING—made easy**

The most advanced and practical textbook on the subject.

J. R. Mitchell, L.I.R.C., A.I.F.S.T.

**THE WINEMAKER'S COOKBOOK**

Gives a whole range of exciting dishes using your home-made wine.

Tilly Timbrell and Bryan Acton

**WINEMAKING AND BREWING**

The theory and practice of winemaking and brewing in detail.

Dr. F. W. Beech and Dr. A. Pollard

**GROWING GRAPES IN BRITAIN**

Indispensible handbook for winemakers whether they have six vines or six thousand.

Gillian Pearkes

**'AMATEUR WINEMAKER" RECIPES**

Fascinatingly varied collection of over 200 recipes.

C. J. J. Berry

## EXPRESS WINEMAKING

How to make delightful wines from fruit in three weeks.

**Ren Bellis**


## PRESERVING WINEMAKING INGREDIENTS

Includes drying, chunk bottling, deep freezing, chemica preservation, etc.

**T. Edwin Belt**


## HOME BREWING SIMPLIFIED

Detailed recipes for bottled and draught beer plus knowhow.

**Dean Jones**


## RECIPES FOR PRIZEWINNING WINES

Produce superb wines for your own satisfaction!

**Bryan Acton**


## WHYS AND WHEREFORES OF WINEMAKING

Assists the winemaker to *understand* what he is doing.

**Cedric Austin**


## HOW TO MAKE WINES WITH A SPARKLE

Discover the secrets of producing Champagne-like wine of superb quality.

**J. Restall and D. Hebbs**

## 130 NEW WINEMAKING RECIPES

Superb collection of up-to-date recipes

C. J. J. Berry

## MAKING WINES LIKE THOSE YOU BUY

Imitate commercial wines at a fraction of what they would cost to buy.

Bryan Acton and Peter Duncan

## BREWING BEERS LIKE THOSE YOU BUY

Over 100 original recipes to enable you to imitate famous beers from all over the world.

Dave Line

## THE GOOD WINES OF EUROPE

A simple guide to the names, types and qualities of wine.

Cedric Austin

## ADVANCED HOME BREWING

The most advanced book on home brewing available in this country.

Ken Shales

## INSTANT WINEMAKING

Simple day to day instructions how to make wines in 3-6 weeks.

Brian Leverett

## PROGRESSIVE WINEMAKING

500 pages, from scientific theory to the production of quality wines at home.

**Peter Duncan and Bryan Acton**


## HOME BREWED BEERS AND STOUTS

The first and still recognised as the best book on this fascinating subject.

**C. J. J. Berry**


## WOODWORK FOR WINEMAKERS

Make your own wine press, fermentation cupboard, fruit pulper, bottle racks, etc.

**C. J. Dart and D. A. Smith**


## BREWING BETTER BEERS

Explains many finer points of brewing technique.

**Ken Shales**


## HINTS ON HOME BREWING

Concise and basic down to earth instructions on home brewing.

**C. J. J. Berry**


## MAKING MEAD

The only full-length paperback available on this winemaking speciality.

**Bryan Acton and Peter Duncan**

**WORLDWIDE WINE RECIPES**

A fascinating look at exotic recipes worldwide.

**Roy Ekins**


**PLANTS UNSAFE FOR WINEMAKING**

—includes native and naturalised plants, shrubs and trees.

**T. Edwin Belt**


**GROWING VINES**

Down-to-earth book for the viticulturalist.

**N. Poulter**


**DURDEN PARK BEER CIRCLE BOOK OF RECIPES**

How to make a whole range of superb beers.

**Wilf Newsom**


**JUDGING HOME-MADE WINES**

National Guild of Judges official handbook.